SANJEEV KAPOOR

Noodles & Rice

In association with Alyona Kapoor

Popular Prakashan
www.popularprakashan.com

Published by
POPULAR PRAKASHAN PVT. LTD.
301, Mahalaxmi Chambers
22, Bhulabhai Desai Road
Mumbai - 400 026
for KHANA KHAZANA PUBLICATIONS PVT. LTD.

First Published 2013

(4320)
ISBN: 978-81-7991-761-9

Design: Anjali Sawant
Photography: Bharat Bhirangi, Dilip Yande and Swapnil Naik

PRINTED IN INDIA
by H. T. Media Limited
B - 2, Sector - 63, Noida

CONTENTS

RICE

Vegetarian Recipes

Non-Vegetarian Recipes

AUTHOR'S NOTE

All over the world, and in India too, rice symbolises prosperity and fertility. The most common form of rice is the simple steamed or boiled rice. More elaborate and exotic dishes have developed over time as local spices and ingredients were added. The humble grain has taken on a luxurious garb, cloaked in aromatic flavours and enriched with among other ingredients, yogurt, butter, legumes, vegetable, meats and seafood.

Over the years, noodles have become an integral part of an urban meals, be it the instant variety, or authentic Chinese noodles. Chinese noodles are made from *moong* beans, rice, wheat and eggs and come in a variety of textures, lengths and shapes. Those made from *moong* beans, also called cellophane noodles, are thread-like and slippery and are cooked by just soaking in hot water. You can put them in soups and stir-fries, just steam them, or even fry them to a crisp! Egg noodles are made by mixing wheat flour, water and eggs and are recognisably yellow.

In *Noodles and Rice*, I have put together a collection of delectable vegetarian and non-vegetarian noodle and rice dishes. Slurp on delicious Chicken Noodle Soup, savour Spicy Noodles with Seafood, try out flavoursome Chilli-Lemon Stewed Vegetables with Noodles, the hearty Brinjal Pulao, the light Thengai Sadham, the healthy Brown Rice Vegetable Pilaf, and the exotic Nasi Lamek, to name a few.

Happy Cooking!

Thai Green Curry Noodle Soup

1½ tablespoons Thai Green Curry Paste (page 94)

200 grams noodles, boiled

2 tablespoons oil

½ small broccoli, separated into small florets

½ cup corn kernels

1 medium carrot, cut into diamonds

1 medium red capsicum, cut into ½-inch triangles

4-5 button mushrooms, sliced

2 cups Vegetable Stock (page 94)

Salt to taste

1 teaspoon lemon juice

1 cup fresh Coconut Milk (page 93)

½ cup bean sprouts

1 fresh red chilli, diagonally sliced

3-4 fresh basil leaves

- Heat the oil in a non-stick pan. Add the broccoli, corn kernels, carrot, red capsicum and mushrooms and sauté for a minute.
- Add the green curry paste and mix well. Add the vegetable stock and salt and cook till the vegetables are tender. Take care that the vegetables are not overcooked.
- Add the lemon juice and coconut milk and mix. Let it heat through.

- Place a ring mould in the centre of soup bowls and pack it with the boiled noodles.
- Pour the soup into the soup bowl around the ring mould.
- Sprinkle bean sprouts.
- Slowly remove the ring mould so as not to disturb the noodles.
- Sprinkle red chilli over the noodles and place the basil leaves on top.
- Serve immediately.

Secret Noodles

2 packets instant noodles with seasoning

1 medium carrot, cut into small cubes

¼ cup green peas, blanched

1 medium tomato, puréed

Salt to taste

50 grams processed cheese, cut into ½-inch cubes

Toothpicks, as required

- Heat three cups of water in a non-stick pan; add the noodles, carrot, half the green peas and the seasoning, and bring to a boil.
- Add the tomato purée and salt if required, and cook until the noodles are tender and the moisture has been absorbed.
- Thread the cheese cubes and remaining green peas alternately onto toothpicks.
- Serve the noodles in deep bowls garnished with cheese-n-pea toothpicks.

Oodles Of Noodles

200 grams noodles

Salt to taste

1 tablespoon oil

2 spring onions, sliced

1 small yellow capsicum, sliced

1 small red capsicum, sliced

4-5 French beans, sliced diagonally and blanched

½ cup sweetcorn kernels, boiled

2 teaspoons soy sauce

2 tablespoons hot and sweet tomato ketchup

1 tablespoon sweet chilli sauce

¼ cup bean sprouts

2 spring onion green stalks, sliced

- Boil the noodles in plenty of salted water. Drain, refresh in cold water and set aside.
- Heat the oil in a non-stick pan; add the spring onions and stir-fry for a while. Add the capsicums and French beans and stir-fry for a few minutes.
- Add the sweetcorn and soy sauce and mix well. Add the noodles and salt and toss to mix.
- Add the hot and sweet tomato ketchup and sweet chilli sauce and mix gently.
- Add the bean sprouts and spring onion greens and mix well. Serve hot.

Quick Stir-Fried Noodles

200 grams eggless noodles
Salt to taste
3 tablespoons oil
1 medium onion, sliced
1 medium carrot, cut into thin strips
¼ medium cabbage, shredded
1 medium green capsicum, cut into thin strips
2 spring onion green stalks, sliced diagonally
1½ tablespoons light soy sauce
1 cup bean sprouts
1 teaspoon sesame oil

- Boil the noodles in six to eight cups of salted water to which one tablespoon of oil has been added; cook till *al dente* (cooked but firm to the bite). Drain, refresh in cold water and drain again. Spread on a large plate to cool.
- Heat two tablespoons of oil in a non-stick wok to smoking point. Add the onion and stir-fry for one minute. Add the carrot, cabbage and capsicum and stir-fry for two to three minutes.
- Add the noodles and salt; stir and toss for one more minute. Add the spring onion greens and soy sauce and toss again. Add the bean sprouts and toss well.
- Transfer the noodles to a serving bowl, sprinkle sesame oil over and serve immediately.

Crisp Noodles With Stir-Fried Vegetables

200 grams eggless noodles

2 medium carrots, cut into ½-inch diamonds

2 medium green capsicums, cut into ½-inch diamonds

½ small head broccoli, separated into small florets

6 pieces of baby corn, sliced diagonally

Salt to taste

3 tablespoons oil + for deep-frying

2-3 garlic cloves, finely chopped

1 inch ginger, finely chopped

1 medium onion, sliced

1 celery stalk, finely chopped

1 fresh red chilli, sliced diagonally

1 tablespoon dark soy sauce

½ teaspoon white pepper powder

½ teaspoon MSG (optional)

2¼ cups Vegetable Stock (page 94)

2 tablespoons cornflour

¼ cup bean sprouts

- Boil the noodles in six to eight cups of salted water to which one tablespoon of oil has been added; cook till *al dente* (cooked but firm to the bite).
- Drain, refresh in cold water, drain again and spread on a large plate to cool.

- Heat sufficient oil in a non-stick wok and deep-fry noodles till crisp and golden brown. Drain on absorbent paper.
- Heat two tablespoons of oil in a non-stick wok; add the garlic and ginger, and sauté on moderate heat for half a minute.
- Add the onion, celery and chilli, and continue to sauté for another minute.
- Add the carrots, capsicums, broccoli and baby corns; sauté on high heat for two to three minutes, stirring and tossing continuously.
- Add the soy sauce, white pepper powder, MSG and salt to taste, and sauté for one minute. Stir in the vegetable stock and bring to a boil.
- Mix the cornflour with three tablespoons of water and stir into the vegetables.
- Simmer for two to three minutes, stirring continuously till sauce is thick and clear. Add the bean sprouts and toss to mix.
- Arrange the fried noodles in a serving plate or a large bowl, spoon the vegetables on top and serve immediately.

Hakka-Style Rice Noodles

150 grams rice noodles

Salt to taste

4 tablespoons oil

1 medium onion, sliced

1 small carrot, cut into thin strips

1 medium green capsicum, cut into thin strips

6-8 French beans, cut into thin strips

¼ small cabbage, finely shredded

1 tablespoon light soy sauce

¼ teaspoon MSG (optional)

¼ teaspoon white pepper powder

½ cup bean sprouts

1 spring onion green stalk, cut into thin long strips

- Boil six cups of water in a deep non-stick pan. Add the salt and one tablespoon of oil. Add the noodles; take the pan off the heat, cover and leave to stand for three minutes.
- Drain the noodles, refresh in cold water and drain again. Spread on a large plate to cool.
- Heat the remaining oil in a non-stick wok; add the onion and stir-fry for two minutes.
- Add the carrot, green capsicum, French beans and cabbage and stir-fry for two minutes, stirring and tossing continuously.

- Add the noodles, soy sauce, MSG, salt to taste and white pepper powder; cook on high heat for a couple of minutes, tossing continuously, until noodles are heated through.
- Add the bean sprouts mix well and serve hot, garnished with spring onion greens.

Five-Spice Stir-Fry

1 teaspoon five-spice powder
200 grams noodles, boiled
1 tablespoon cornflour
1 cup orange juice
4 tablespoons oil
5-6 garlic cloves, chopped
8-10 French beans, diagonally sliced
1 medium carrot, sliced
8-10 broccoli florets
1 medium onion, sliced
Salt to taste
1 tablespoon soy sauce
2 teaspoons crushed red chillies
7-8 fresh button mushrooms, quartered
½ tablespoon honey
¼ teaspoon MSG (optional)

- Mix the cornflour with the orange juice.
- Heat two tablespoons of oil in a non-stick wok. Add the garlic and sauté for half a minute. Add the French beans, carrot and broccoli and stir-fry for two to three minutes.
- Add the onion, salt, soy sauce, half the crushed red chillies and five-spice powder, and continue to stir-fry for three to four minutes.

- Add the mushrooms, honey and MSG. Stir in the cornflour-orange juice mixture and cook till thick.
- Heat the remaining oil in a separate non-stick pan.
- Add the boiled noodles and stir-fry for two minutes.
- Transfer the noodles to a plate. Pour the sauce over and sprinkle the remaining crushed red chillies on top. Serve hot.

Chilli-Lemon Stewed Vegetables With Noodles

2 green chillies, sliced

2 stalks lemon grass, chopped

1 tablespoon lemon juice

7-8 cauliflower florets, sliced finely

7-8 fresh button mushrooms, sliced

¼ cup corn kernels

1 small green capsicum,
cut into ½-inch pieces

½ medium red capsicum
cut into ½-inch pieces

½ medium yellow capsicum
cut into ½-inch pieces

¼ cup noodles, boiled

3 tablespoons oil

¼ cup bean sprouts

2 medium tomatoes,
cut into 1-inch pieces

4 cups Vegetable Stock (page 94)

1 teaspoon cornflour

Salt to taste

5-6 black peppercorns, crushed

- Heat one tablespoon of oil in a non-stick wok. Add the noodles and sauté till lightly brown. Remove onto a serving dish and keep warm.

- Heat the remaining oil in the same wok. Add the green chillies and lemon grass and sauté for a minute.
- Add the cauliflower, mushrooms, corn kernels, capsicums, bean sprouts and tomatoes and stir.
- Add the vegetable stock and mix. Bring the mixture to a boil.
- Add the cornflour mixed in one tablespoon of water and stir. Cook till the mixture thickens slightly.
- Add the salt, crushed peppercorns and lemon juice and mix gently.
- Pour over the noodles and serve hot.

Vegetable Hakka Noodles

400 grams noodles

6 tablespoons oil

1 medium onion, sliced

1 medium carrot, cut into thin strips

1 medium green capsicum, cut into thin strips

¼ small cabbage, finely shredded

1 tablespoon soy sauce

¼ teaspoon MSG (optional)

Salt to taste

¼ teaspoon white pepper powder

1 cup bean sprouts

1 spring onion green stalk, finely shredded

- Boil the noodles in sufficient water. Drain and cool.
- Heat the oil in a non-stick wok; add the onion and stir-fry for two minutes. Add the carrot, capsicum and cabbage and stir-fry for two minutes, stirring and tossing continuously.
- Add the noodles, soy sauce, MSG, salt to taste and white pepper powder and cook on high heat for a couple of minutes or until the noodles are heated through, tossing continuously.
- Add the bean sprouts, mix well and serve hot garnished with spring onion greens.

Singapore Noodles

200 grams rice noodles

Salt to taste

1 tablespoon oil

4 tablespoons Chilli Oil (page 93)

1 inch ginger, chopped

3-4 garlic cloves, chopped

¼ small cabbage, finely shredded

1 small carrot, grated

1 medium green capsicum, cut into thin strips

2 spring onions, sliced

½ tablespoon light soy sauce

3 tablespoons tomato sauce

¼ teaspoon MSG (optional)

½ teaspoon white pepper powder

½ cup bean sprouts

1 tablespoon white vinegar

- Boil six cups of water in a deep non-stick pan. Add salt and one tablespoon of oil. Add the noodles; take the pan off the heat, cover and leave to stand for three minutes.
- Drain the noodles, refresh in cold water and drain again. Spread on a large plate to cool.
- Heat the chilli oil in a non-stick wok; add the ginger and garlic and stir-fry for one minute. Add the cabbage, carrot and

capsicum and continue to stir-fry for one minute. Add the spring onions, reserving some greens for garnishing, and cook on high heat for one minute more.

- Add the noodles, soy sauce, tomato sauce, MSG, white pepper powder and salt to taste.
- Mix well and cook for a couple of minutes, tossing and stirring continuously.
- Add the bean sprouts and vinegar and toss well.
- Serve hot, garnished with reserved spring onion greens.

Chicken Noodle Soup

300 grams rice noodles or rice vermicelli
2 fresh red chillies, seeded and sliced
2 tablespoons soy sauce
1¼ cups bean sprouts, blanched
1 medium onion, sliced
White pepper powder to taste
10-12 fresh basil leaves
2 tablespoons chopped fresh coriander
1 lemon, cut into wedges

Broth
10 cups Chicken Stock (page 93)
500 grams boneless chicken, cubed
1 inch cinnamon
2-3 spring onion green stalks, sliced
1 inch ginger, crushed
2 teaspoons sugar
Salt to taste
2 tablespoons fish sauce

- Place the sliced red chillies in a bowl and add the soy sauce. Set aside.
- For the broth, pour the chicken stock into a deep non-stick pan. Add the chicken cubes, cinnamon, spring onions, ginger, sugar and salt, and bring to a boil over high heat.

- Lower heat and simmer for forty-five minutes, skimming the scum off as it rises to the surface.
- Add the fish sauce and remove from heat. Remove the chicken with a slotted spoon and set aside to cool. Strain the broth and keep warm over very low heat.
- Boil plenty of water in a deep non-stick pan. Add the noodles and blanch for about five minutes or until they soften. If using vermicelli it will take around two minutes.
- Drain and rinse in cold water. Drain again thoroughly and set aside.
- When the chicken cools completely, shred into thin strips.
- Place the noodles/vermicelli in individual serving bowls, top with bean sprouts, shredded chicken and onion. Pour the hot broth into the bowls.
- Sprinkle with white pepper powder; garnish with the basil and chopped coriander. Serve piping hot, with the lemon wedges and the bowl of red chillies in soy sauce on the side.

Chiang Mai Noodles

100 grams rice noodles, boiled and drained

500 grams chicken thigh meat, cut into ½-inch cubes

1 cup thick Coconut Milk (page 93)

2-3 garlic cloves, crushed

4-5 white peppercorns, crushed

2 tablespoons chopped fresh coriander

1 teaspoon Red Curry Paste (page 94)

2 tablespoons dark soy sauce

2 red capsicums, chopped

2½ cups Chicken Stock (page 93)

Salt to taste

1½ tablespoons cornflour

Garnish

100 grams rice noodles, fried

2 garlic cloves, fried and chopped

2 tablespoons chopped fresh coriander

2 lemons, cut into wedges

- Pour the coconut milk into a large non-stick wok and bring to a boil over medium heat. Continue to boil for ten minutes, stirring continuously, until the milk separates and an oily layer appears on the surface.
- Add the garlic, white peppercorns, chopped coriander and red curry paste.

- Cook, stirring continuously, for a few seconds, until fragrant.
- Add the chicken cubes and toss over high heat until glossy.
- Add the soy sauce and red capsicums and stir-fry for three or four minutes.
- Pour in the stock and bring to a boil. Lower heat and simmer for ten to fifteen minutes, or until the chicken is cooked. Add salt to taste.
- Add the cornflour mixed with half a cup of water and cook for two minutes.
- Place the boiled rice noodles into warmed individual serving bowls.
- Ladle portions of chicken over the noodles and top with the fried noodles, fried garlic and chopped coriander.
- Serve hot with lemon wedges.

Noodles, Chicken and Prawns in Coconut Broth (recipe on page 32)

Noodles, Chicken And Prawns In Coconut Broth

200 grams rice noodles, soaked in cold water

125 grams boneless chicken, cooked and shredded

175 grams large prawns, cooked

1 cup Coconut Milk (page 93)

1 medium onion, quartered

½ inch ginger, sliced

2 garlic cloves

4 almonds

1 fresh red chilli, seeded

2 inches lemon grass stalk, bruised and chopped

1 inch fresh turmeric, sliced

½ tablespoon roasted coriander seeds

½ teaspoon roasted cumin seeds

2 tablespoons oil

3½ cups Chicken Stock (page 93)

Salt to taste

Black pepper powder to taste

2 hard-boiled eggs, quartered

1 stalk spring onion greens, shredded

1 large onion, sliced and deep-fried

- Grind together the onion, ginger, garlic, almonds, fresh red chilli, lemon grass and fresh turmeric to a fine paste.

- Grind the coriander and cumin seeds coarsely and add to the ground paste.
- Heat the oil in a deep non-stick pan. Add the spice mixture and sauté without browning till fragrant.
- Add the coconut milk, chicken stock, salt and pepper powder. Bring the mixture to a boil, lower heat and simmer for ten minutes.
- Meanwhile drain the noodles and plunge them into a large pan of boiling salted water for two minutes. Drain in a colander and rinse in cold water.
- Add the prawns to the soup cooking in the pan and let the mixture come to a boil.
- Divide the noodles among individual bowls. Top with soup, eggs and chicken. Sprinkle spring onion greens and deep-fried onion and serve hot.

CHICKEN CHOWMEIN

1 boneless chicken breast, boiled and shredded

200 grams egg noodles

1 teaspoon salt

¼ cup oil

8 baby corn cobs, halved

1 egg, beaten

2-3 garlic cloves, sliced

1 inch ginger, chopped

1 medium onion, peeled and sliced

6 fresh button mushrooms, halved

1 medium red capsicum, seeded and cut into thin strips

2 teaspoons light soy sauce

1 teaspoon sesame oil

1 tablespoon toasted sesame seeds

- Place a deep non-stick pan over medium heat and add six cups of water, half a teaspoon salt and one tablespoon oil and bring it to boil.
- Add the noodles and cook for eight minutes or till almost done. Drain into a colander. Refresh in cold water, drain again and spread on a large plate to cool.
- Place another non-stick pan over medium heat and add one cup of water and bring

it to a boil. Add the baby corn and blanch in boiling water for two minutes.

- Drain in a colander, refresh in cold water and set aside.
- Place a non-stick frying pan on medium heat and pour in one teaspoon oil. Add the beaten egg and stir to scramble it. When done set aside in a small bowl.
- Place a non-stick wok over medium heat and pour the remaining oil; add the garlic, ginger and onion and sauté for two to three minutes.
- Add the baby corn, mushrooms and capsicum and sauté for two to three minutes. Add the chicken and continue to sauté for one minute more.
- Add the soy sauce and remaining salt and stir well.
- Add the noodles and sesame oil and toss. Add the scrambled egg and toss again.
- Reduce heat to low and cook for two to three minutes or until the noodles are heated through. Transfer into a serving bowl.
- Serve hot, garnished with toasted sesame seeds.

Hot And Sweet Fried Noodles

200 grams rice vermicelli or rice noodles, soaked

Oil for deep-frying

Sauce

2 tablespoons oil

200 grams bean curd (tofu), cut into thin strips

8 garlic cloves, finely chopped

8 spring onions, finely chopped

½ tablespoon light soy sauce

1 tablespoon palm sugar or light brown sugar

1½ cups Vegetable Stock (page 94)

1 tablespoon lemon juice

2 teaspoons red chilli flakes

Garnish

3 tablespoons oil

4 eggs, lightly beaten with 4 tablespoons water

1 cup bean sprouts

4 spring onions, thinly shredded

2 fresh red chillies, seeded and finely chopped

- Heat sufficient oil in a non-stick wok and deep-fry vermicelli or noodles till golden and crisp. Drain on an absorbent paper.
- To make the sauce, heat the oil in a non-stick wok. Add the bean curd and cook over medium heat until crisp. Drain on absorbent paper and transfer onto a plate.
- Add the garlic and spring onions to the oil remaining in the wok and stir-fry till golden brown.
- Add the soy sauce, sugar, vegetable stock, lemon juice and chilli flakes. Cook, stirring, until the mixture begins to caramelise.
- Add the bean curd and stir until it has soaked up some of the liquid. Take the wok off the heat and set aside.
- To prepare the garnish, heat the oil in a non-stick pan.
- Pour in the eggs in a thin stream to form trails. As soon as the eggs set, lift them out and place on a plate.
- Crumble the noodles into the tofu sauce and mix well. Spoon this mixture into warmed serving bowls.
- Sprinkle with bean sprouts, spring onion, fried egg strips, red chillies and serve immediately.

Burnt Garlic Chopsuey

12-15 garlic cloves, sliced lengthways

300 grams egg noodles

6 tablespoons oil + for deep-frying

4 eggs

1 inch ginger, grated

100 grams boneless chicken, cut into thin strips

1 medium onion, finely sliced

½ medium carrot, grated

3-4 French beans, cut diagonally into thin strips

¼ small cabbage, shredded

½ cup tomato sauce

½ tablespoon light soy sauce

½ teaspoon white pepper powder

¼ teaspoon MSG (optional)

Salt to taste

½ medium green capsicum, cut into thin strips

2 cups Chicken Stock (page 93)

2 tablespoons cornflour

1 tablespoon white vinegar

½ cup bean sprouts

- Boil the noodles until almost cooked, drain and cool.
- Heat sufficient oil in a non-stick wok and deep-fry the noodles till crisp and golden. Drain on absorbent paper.

Divide the fried noodles into four equal portions and keep warm on separate shallow plates or serving platters.

- Heat half a tablespoon of oil in a non-stick pan; break an egg into the pan and cook for half a minute on both sides. Do the same with the rest of the eggs.
- Mix cornflour and half a cup of water.
- Heat four tablespoons of oil in a non-stick wok; add the garlic and sauté till almost burnt. Reserve half a teaspoon of garlic for garnishing.
- Add the ginger to the sautéed garlic and stir-fry for a few seconds. Add the chicken strips and cook for half a minute.
- Add the onion, carrot, French beans and cabbage and continue to stir-fry for one minute more.
- Stir in the tomato sauce, soy sauce, white pepper powder, MSG, salt to taste, capsicum and chicken stock.
- Cook for two minutes, and stir in the cornflour mixed in half a cup of water. Continue to cook for one minute, or until the sauce thickens, stirring continuously.
- Add the vinegar and bean sprouts; stir well and ladle over each portion of fried noodles.
- Top with reserved sautéed garlic and a fried egg. Serve immediately.

Spicy Noodles with Seafood (recipe on page 42)

Spicy Noodles With Seafood

6-8 mussels or clams

2 medium crabs

100 grams boneless fish fillets, cut into 1-inch pieces

12 small prawns, peeled and deveined

300 grams flat noodles

6 tablespoons oil

6-8 garlic cloves, chopped

1 inch ginger, chopped

1 medium onion, sliced

½ medium green capsicum, cut into thin strips

1 tablespoon light soy sauce

1 tablespoon oyster sauce

2 tablespoons chilli-garlic sauce

½ teaspoon white pepper powder

¼ teaspoon MSG (optional)

Salt to taste

1 tablespoon lemon juice

1 stalk spring onion greens, finely chopped

- Open the mussel or clam shells with a knife and scoop out the meat.
- Boil the crabs in two cups of water for three to four minutes. Cool, separate the claws, crack them lightly and set aside. Remove meat from the rest of the crab.

- Boil the flat noodles in seven to eight cups of water.
- Drain, refresh in cold water and cool.
- Heat the oil in a non-stick wok; add the garlic, ginger and onion and stir-fry for a few seconds.
- Add the prawns, fish, mussels or clams and capsicum and continue to stir-fry for one minute.
- Add the noodles, crab meat and claws, soy sauce, oyster sauce, chilli-garlic sauce, white pepper powder, MSG and salt to taste.
- Cook on high heat for a couple of minutes, tossing continuously.
- Mix in lemon juice and serve hot, garnished with spring onion greens.

Singapore Noodle Rice

¾ cup rice

100 grams noodles

12 small prawns, shelled

200 grams boneless chicken, cut into thin strips

4 tablespoons chilli oil

1 inch ginger, finely chopped

3-4 garlic cloves, finely chopped

2 spring onions, finely chopped

2 eggs, lightly whisked

½ tablespoon soy sauce

3 tablespoons tomato sauce

¼ teaspoon MSG (optional)

½ teaspoon white pepper powder

Salt to taste

1 tablespoon vinegar

- Soak the rice in four to five cups of water for an hour. Cook in sufficient boiling water until just cooked. Remove, drain well and cool.
- Boil the noodles in sufficient water. Drain, remove and cool.
- Devein, wash thoroughly and pat dry prawns with an absorbent kitchen towel. Set aside.
- Heat chilli oil in a non-stick wok; add the ginger and garlic and stir-fry briefly.

- Add the prawns and chicken and continue to stir-fry for half a minute.
- Add the chopped spring onions reserving some for garnishing and cook on high heat for a minute more.
- Stir in the whisked egg and continue to cook on high heat for half a minute or until the egg is scrambled.
- Add the noodles, rice, soy sauce, tomato sauce, MSG, white pepper powder and salt to taste.
- Mix well and cook for a couple of minutes until noodles and rice are heated through, tossing continuously.
- Mix in vinegar and serve hot, garnished with reserved chopped spring onion greens.

Fried Jasmine Rice With Basil

4 cups cooked Jasmine rice

15-20 basil leaves, roughly chopped

3 tablespoons oil

1 medium onion, chopped

7-8 garlic cloves, chopped

1 tablespoon Red Curry Paste (page 94)

¼ cup shelled green peas, blanched

½ head of broccoli, separated into small florets, blanched

1 large carrot, diced and blanched

Salt to taste

White pepper powder to taste

2 spring onion green stalks, chopped

- Heat two tablespoons of oil in a non-stick wok; add the onion and garlic and sauté for two or three minutes.
- Add the red curry paste, mix well and sauté for two minutes.
- Add the rice, green peas, broccoli, carrot, salt, white pepper powder and toss well to mix.

- Stir in the spring onion greens and basil leaves.
- Serve hot with a spicy Thai curry.

Chef's Tip

As Jasmine rice is not easily available, use Basmati rice. Add around twenty to twenty-five jasmine flowers tied in a *potli* to the water in which the rice is cooked.

Brinjal Pulao

Vangi Bhaat

8-10 baby brinjals

1½ cups rice

4 tablespoons + 1 teaspoon oil

1 teaspoon mustard seeds

6 dried red chillies

1 sprig curry leaves

1 tablespoon split Bengal gram, soaked and drained

2 medium onions, sliced

4 green chillies, slit

½ teaspoon turmeric powder

A pinch of asafoetida

Salt to taste

1½ tablespoons Tamarind Pulp (recipe follows)

Masala Powder

2 teaspoons oil

8-10 black peppercorns

4 dried red chillies

½ teaspoon fennel seeds

1 tablespoon poppy seeds

2 cloves

2 green cardamoms

- Wash and boil rice in plenty of water till three-fourth done. Drain well, mix two tablespoons of oil and set aside to cool.
- Cut the brinjals into four keeping the stem intact.

- For the *masala* powder, heat two teaspoons of oil in a non-stick pan and lightly fry peppercorns, red chillies, fennel seeds, poppy seeds, cloves and cardamoms. Cool and grind to a coarse powder.
- Heat the remaining oil and add the mustard seeds, red chillies, curry leaves and drained split Bengal gram. Fry till well-roasted and light brown in colour. Add the onions and sauté till lightly coloured. Add the green chillies and stir.
- Add the brinjals and stir-fry on high heat till it is half done. Sprinkle the turmeric powder, asafoetida and salt. Mix and add the tamarind pulp. Add the *masala* powder and cook till the brinjals are almost done.
- Mix the rice into this thoroughly and toss over high heat. Reduce heat, sprinkle two tablespoons of water, cover and cook till the rice is soft and completely cooked.

Chef's Tip

You can substitute tamarind with lemon juice,
but add the lemon juice after the rice is fully cooked.

Tamarind Pulp

Soak 75 grams tamarind in 100 ml warm water for 10-15 minutes. Grind to a smooth paste and strain to remove any fibres. Store in an airtight container in the refrigerator.

Cauliflower And Lemon Rice

300 grams cauliflower, separated into small florets
2 tablespoons lemon juice
2 cups cooked Basmati rice
1½ teaspoons salt
A pinch of sugar
4 green chillies, roughly chopped
3 dried red chillies, broken into 2 pieces
2 tablespoons coriander seeds
5-6 cashew nuts, roughly chopped
¼ teaspoon turmeric powder
1 teaspoon oil
¼ teaspoon mustard seeds
½ teaspoon skinless split black gram
⅛ teaspoon fenugreek seeds
A pinch of asafoetida
7–8 curry leaves

- Place a deep non-stick pan on medium heat and pour in four cups of water and bring it to a boil.
- Add the cauliflower florets and cook for five to six minutes. Drain into a colander and set aside.
- Place the lemon juice in a small bowl. Add the salt and sugar and stir till dissolved. Set aside.

- Grind together the green chilles, red chillies, coriander seeds, cashew nuts and turmeric powder with four tablespoons of water to a fine paste in a blender.
- Heat the oil in a non-stick *kadai* on medium heat.
- Add the mustard seeds, split black gram and fenugreek seeds and sauté until the black gram turns light brown.
- Add the asafoetida and curry leaves and sauté for thirty seconds.
- Add the ground paste and cauliflower and stir well. Add the rice and lemon juice mixture and stir lightly.
- Reduce heat to low, cover the wok with a lid and cook for five minutes.
- Serve hot.

Brown Rice Vegetable Pilaf

1½ cups brown rice

2 medium carrots, cut into ½-inch small pieces

10-12 French beans, cut into ½-inch pieces

¼ medium cauliflower, cut into small florets

6-7 medium fresh button mushrooms, halved (optional)

½ cup green peas, shelled and blanched

1 bay leaf

2-3 cloves

1 teaspoon cumin seeds

1 inch cinnamon

Salt to taste

2 green chillies, slit

2 tablespoons fresh coriander, finely chopped

- Soak the brown rice in four to five cups of water for two hours.
- Drain and set aside.
- Heat a deep non-stick pan; add the bay leaf, cloves, cumin seeds and cinnamon and roast for a few seconds or till a nice aroma is given out.

- Add the drained rice and salt and roast for one to two minutes. Add four cups of water. Bring it to a boil.
- Add the carrots, French beans, cauliflower, mushrooms and green chillies.
- Stir and bring to a boil. Reduce heat, cover and cook till almost done.
- Add the green peas and mix gently. Cover and cook till done.
- Serve hot garnished with chopped coriander.

Chef's Tip

The dish becomes a little sticky on cooking.

Kashmiri Pulao

250 grams cottage cheese, cut into ½-inch cubes

1½ cups Basmati rice

A few saffron threads

Oil for deep-frying

2 medium onions, sliced

3 black cardamoms

2 bay leaves

3 cloves

2 one-inch cinnamon sticks

½ teaspoon dried ginger powder

1 teaspoon fennel seeds

¼ teaspoon asafoetida

Salt to taste

3 tablespoons ghee

1 teaspoon cumin seeds

3-4 green cardamoms

10-12 raisins

8 cashew nuts, halved

- Soak the rice in three cups of water for half an hour. Drain. Soak the saffron in two teaspoons of water.
- Heat the oil in a non-stick *kadai* and deep-fry the onions till golden and crisp. Drain on absorbent paper. Set aside.
- Bring four and a half cups of water, black cardamoms, bay leaves, cloves,

cinnamon, dried ginger powder, fennel seeds, asafoetida and salt to a boil.

- Lower heat and simmer for fifteen to twenty minutes or till reduced to three cups of stock.
- Remove from heat and strain the stock. Discard the spices.
- Heat the ghee in a deep non-stick pan; add the cumin seeds and cardamoms. When the cumin seeds change colour; add the drained rice and the stock.
- Bring to a boil, lower heat, cover and cook till the rice is almost done. Gently stir in the cottage cheese cubes, raisins and cashew nuts.
- Sprinkle the saffron and fried onions over the rice. Cook on *dum* for another eight to ten minutes. Serve hot.

Imli Chawal

4 tablespoons Tamarind Pulp (page 49)

1½ cups rice, soaked

¼ teaspoon turmeric powder

Salt to taste

2 tablespoons oil

½ teaspoon mustard seeds

1 teaspoon skinless split black gram

1 teaspoon split Bengal gram

A large pinch of asafoetida

10-15 curry leaves

2 green chillies, finely chopped

2 dried red chillies, broken

½ cup crushed roasted peanuts

1 teaspoon roasted sesame seeds

- Cook the rice with the turmeric powder, salt and three cups of water till done. Ensure that the rice grains remain separate. Spread out on a plate to cool.
- Heat the oil in a non-stick pan. Add the mustard seeds, split black gram and split Bengal gram and sauté till the gram turn golden.
- Add the asafoetida, curry leaves, green chillies and red chillies and sauté till fragrant. Add the tamarind pulp diluted in one-fourth cup of water and mix. Cook till the mixture thickens.
- Add the rice and mix gently. Adjust the salt. Add the peanuts and sesame seeds and mix gently. Serve hot.

Chef's Tip: This rice will keep for three to four days and is ideal to carry while travelling.

Aloo Palak Pulao

2 medium potatoes, cut into ¾-inch cubes

1 cup finely chopped spinach

1½ cups rice, soaked

¼ medium bottle gourd, peeled and cut into ¾-inch cubes

2 tablespoons ghee

1 teaspoon cumin seeds

1 medium tomato, finely chopped

Salt to taste

- Heat the ghee in a deep non-stick pan and add the cumin seeds. When they begin to change colour add the tomato, potatoes and bottle gourd and sauté for two minutes.
- Add the rice and spinach and sauté for two more minutes. Add three cups of hot water and salt and mix.
- When the mixture comes to a boil, reduce heat, cover and cook till the rice and the vegetables are done.
- Serve hot.

Healthy Protein Pulao

1 cup soya granules, soaked in 1 cup water

1½ cups Basmati rice, soaked

2 tablespoons rice bran oil

½ teaspoon cumin seeds

1 inch cinnamon

3-4 cloves

2-3 green cardamoms

3 medium onions, chopped

1 inch ginger, chopped

10 garlic cloves, chopped

1½ tablespoons red chilli powder

¼ teaspoon turmeric powder

1 tablespoon coriander powder

3-4 large tomatoes, chopped

1 cup green peas, parboiled

Salt to taste

2 tablespoons chopped fresh coriander

3 cups Vegetable Stock (page 94)

- Heat the oil in a deep non-stick pan.
- Add the cumin seeds, cinnamon, cloves, cardamoms and onions.
- Sauté for two minutes and add the ginger and garlic and sauté for another minute.
- Add the chilli powder, turmeric powder, coriander powder and continue to sauté.

- Add a little water so that the *masala* does not burn.
- Add the tomatoes and soya granules.
- Cook for a minute and add the green peas, salt and chopped coriander.
- Add the rice and stir. Add three cups of vegetable stock and stir.
- When it comes to a boil, lower the heat, cover and cook till the rice is done.
- Serve hot with *raita*.

KAIKARI BIRYANI

Vegetable Biryani

1½ cups long grained rice, soaked

1 medium tomato, seeded and cubed

1 medium green capsicum, seeded and cubed

1 medium carrot, cubed

2 medium potatoes, cubed

10 French beans, cut into ½-inch pieces

¼ small cauliflower, separated into small florets

¼ cup shelled green peas

8 tablespoons oil

2 medium onions, chopped

10-12 curry leaves

4 green chillies, slit

Salt to taste

¼ cup chopped fresh coriander

8-10 fresh mint leaves, torn

1 tablespoon lemon juice

Masala Paste

2 tablespoons oil

10-12 garlic cloves, roughly chopped

1 inch ginger, roughly chopped

¼ cup grated coconut

4 dried red chillies

2 tablespoons coriander seeds

1 teaspoon cumin seeds

1 tablespoon poppy seeds

2 tablespoons fennel seeds

Garam Masala

½ inch cinnamon

2 cloves

2 green cardamoms

2 mace blades

1 star anise

10-12 black peppercorns

A small pinch of nutmeg powder

- For the *masala* paste, heat the oil in a small non-stick pan or on a non-stick *tawa* and fry all the *masala* ingredients till light brown. Cool and grind to a smooth paste with a little water.
- Dry-roast all the ingredients for the garam *masala* for two to three minutes and pound into a coarse powder.
- Heat the oil in a non-stick pan and sauté the onions till golden brown.
- Add the curry leaves, green chillies and *masala* paste and sauté till the oil separates. Add the tomato and cook over high heat till the moisture evaporates.
- Stir in all the remaining vegetables and cook for a couple of minutes over high heat.
- Drain the rice well and add to the vegetable mixture with salt to taste.
- Add three and a half cups of hot water and bring to a boil over high heat.
- Lower the heat to medium, cover and cook, stirring occasionally, till the rice is almost cooked.

- Sprinkle the chopped coriander and mint, freshly pounded *garam masala* powder and lemon juice. Stir well and cover with a tight-fitting lid.
- Place the pan on hot charcoals for about ten minutes. Uncover the pan when ready to serve.

Chef's Tip

Traditionally *Jeeraga Samba* rice is used to make this *biryani*. But you can also use any other long grained rice.

Thengai Sadham

Coconut Rice

1 cup grated coconut

1½ cups rice, soaked

1 tablespoon pure ghee

6-8 cashew nuts

4 tablespoons oil

½ teaspoon mustard seeds

1 teaspoon skinless split black gram

2 dried red chillies, broken into two

10-12 curry leaves

1 medium onion, finely chopped

2 green chillies, finely chopped

1 inch ginger, finely chopped

Salt to taste

2 tablespoons chopped fresh coriander

1 teaspoon coconut oil (optional)

- Boil sufficient water in a deep non-stick pan and cook the rice, stirring frequently till almost done.
- Drain and spread out on a flat plate to cool.
- Heat the ghee in a small non-stick pan and stir-fry the cashew nuts till light brown and set aside.
- Heat the oil in a non-stick *kadai* and add the mustard seeds.

- When they begin to splutter, add the split black gram, red chillies and curry leaves and sauté for a few seconds.
- Add the onion, green chillies and ginger, and sauté for two to three minutes, or until the onion is translucent.
- Add the coconut and cook over medium heat for two minutes.
- Add the cooked rice, salt and chopped coriander and toss well to mix. Cook till the rice is heated through.
- Drizzle with the coconut oil and mix lightly.
- Serve hot, garnished with the fried cashew nuts.

Lemon Rice With Vegetables

2 tablespoons lemon juice

2 cups cooked rice

1 small carrot, chopped

1 small green capsicum, chopped

2 tablespoons oil

¼ teaspoon mustard seeds

A pinch of asafoetida

2 green chillies, chopped

15-20 curry leaves

2 dried red chillies, broken

1 small onion, finely chopped

¼ teaspoon turmeric powder

¼ cup roasted peanuts, crushed (optional)

Salt to taste

- Heat the oil in a non-stick *kadai*. Add the mustard seeds, asafoetida, green chillies, curry leaves and red chillies. When the mustard seeds splutter add the onion and sauté till translucent.
- Add the carrot and capsicum and sauté for four to five minutes.
- Add the rice, turmeric powder, roasted peanuts (if using), salt and lemon juice and mix well. Cook till the rice is heated through.
- Serve hot.

Makai Ki Khichdi

1 cup corn kernels

1¼ cups rice, soaked

2 tablespoons lemon juice

3 tablespoons ghee

1 teaspoon cumin seeds

A pinch of asafoetida

2 inches ginger, finely chopped

4-5 green chillies, chopped

½ teaspoon turmeric powder

Salt to taste

2 tablespoons chopped fresh coriander

- Boil the corn in two cups of water with lemon juice till tender. Drain and set aside.
- Heat the ghee in a non-stick pan. Add the cumin seeds. When the cumin seeds start to change colour, add the asafoetida, ginger, green chillies and turmeric powder. Mix well and cook for two to three minutes.
- Add the cooked corn and three and a half cups of water and bring to a boil. Add the rice and salt, mix and cook on low heat till the rice is cooked and the khichdi is of the right consistency.
- Garnish with chopped coriander and serve hot with yogurt, papad and pickle of your choice.

Pineapple Fried Rice

3-4 tinned pineapple slices, chopped

1½ cups rice, soaked

Salt to taste

2 tablespoons oil

4 spring onions, chopped

2 green chillies, seeded, chopped

1 small carrot, grated

6-8 French beans, sliced

1 teaspoon soy sauce

¼ teaspoon MSG (optional)

1 fresh red chilli, seeded, sliced

- Cook the rice in four cups of salted boiling water till almost done.
- Drain, refresh in cold water and drain again. Spread on a large plate to cool.
- Heat two tablespoons of oil in a non-stick wok; add the spring onions and green chillies and stir-fry for a minute.
- Add the carrot and French beans and continue to stir-fry for another two minutes.
- Add the rice, soy sauce, MSG and salt and sauté for two minutes stirring and tossing continuously. Add the pineapple and continue to sauté for a minute.
- Garnish with fresh red chilli and serve hot.

Chef's Tip

You can serve this in a scooped out shell of a fresh pineapple.

Soya Granule Rice

1 cup soya granules

1 cup Basmati rice, soaked

3-4 tablespoons ghee

1 inch cinnamon

2-3 green cardamoms

3-4 cloves

½ teaspoon caraway seeds

½ teaspoon cumin seeds

3 medium onions, chopped

1 tablespoon ginger paste

1 tablespoon garlic paste

1 tablespoon coriander powder

¼ teaspoon turmeric powder

1 teaspoon red chilli powder

3-4 large tomatoes, chopped

Salt to taste

2-3 green chillies, chopped

2 tablespoons chopped fresh coriander

½ teaspoon *garam masala* powder

- Soak the soya granules in one cup of milk for half an hour. Set aside.
- Heat the ghee in a thick-bottomed non-stick pan; add the cinnamon, cardamoms, cloves, caraway seeds and cumin seeds.
- When they begin to change colour, add the onions and continue to sauté.

- Add the ginger paste, garlic paste and a little water and continue to sauté for one minute.
- Add the coriander powder, turmeric powder, chilli powder and tomatoes. Mix and sauté for another minute. Add the salt and mix.
- Add the soaked soya granules and green chillies. Cover and cook till dry.
- Add the soaked rice with two cups of water and mix.
- Add the chopped coriander and *garam masala* powder and mix well.
- Cover and cook on low heat till the rice is done. Stir once or twice while the rice is cooking.
- Serve hot with fresh yogurt.

Rainbow Rice

2 cups cooked rice
2 tablespoons oil
1 small carrot, chopped
1 small green capsicum, chopped
¼ cup cabbage, chopped
2 spring onions, chopped
2 teaspoons tomato ketchup
A pinch of black pepper powder
Salt to taste

- Heat the oil in a non-stick wok, add the carrot, capsicum, cabbage and spring onions and sauté for four or five minutes.
- Stir in the rice, tomato ketchup, pepper powder and salt and mix well.
- Serve hot.

Chef's Tip

Add one-fourth cup of hot water just before finishing.
It will keep the fried rice nice and moist and not feel too dry.

Brown Rice Biryani With Chutney Chicken

2 cups brown Basmati rice, soaked

½ cup Green Chutney (page 94)

800 grams chicken on the bone, cut into 1½-inch pieces

Salt to taste

2 inches cinnamon

6 green cardamoms

8 cloves

½ cup yogurt

¼ teaspoon turmeric powder

3 tablespoons oil

2 medium onions, sliced

1 teaspoon ginger paste

1 teaspoon garlic paste

3 tablespoons chopped fresh coriander

5-6 saffron threads, soaked in 2 tablespoons of milk

A few rose petals

A few sprigs of fresh mint leaves

1 cup deep-fried onion slices

1 teaspoon screw pine water

1 teaspoon rose water

½ teaspoon *garam masala* powder

- Drain and cook the brown rice with salt, six cups of water, half the cinnamon, half the cardamoms and half the cloves till three-fourth done. Drain and set aside.

- Place the green chutney in a bowl; add the yogurt, salt, turmeric powder and mix. Marinate the chicken in it for an hour preferably in the refrigerator.
- Heat the oil in a deep non-stick pan; add the remaining cinnamon, remaining cardamoms, remaining cloves and the onions and sauté till the onions turn brown.
- Add the ginger paste, garlic paste and sauté adding a little water to avoid scorching. Add the marinated chicken, mix and cook. Reduce heat, cover and cook for five minutes. Add the chopped coriander and mix.
- In a deep microwave-safe bowl, spread a layer of half the brown rice at the base.
- Sprinkle half the saffron-flavoured milk, rose petals, mint leaves, fried onion slices, screw pine water, rose water and *garam masala* powder. Spread the chicken gravy and again spread layers of the remaining brown rice, saffron-flavoured milk, rose petals, mint leaves, fried onion slices, screw pine water, rose water and *garam masala* powder.
- Cover with a cling wrap, make a few holes on it. Cook on Microwave HIGH (100%) for five minutes.
- Allow standing time of five minutes. Remove the cling wrap and serve hot with a *raita* of your choice.

Chicken Biryani

500 grams chicken on the bone, cut into 1½ inch pieces

1½ cups *sela* (*ukda*) Basmati rice, soaked

1 tablespoon ginger paste

1 tablespoon garlic paste

1 teaspoon green chilli paste

1 tablespoon coriander powder

1 tablespoon roasted cumin powder

1 teaspoon *garam masala* powder

1 teaspoon green cardamom powder

Salt to taste

1 cup yogurt

3 tablespoons oil

1 bay leaf

4 cloves

2 green cardamoms

1 black cardamom

5 cups Chicken Stock (page 93)

A few saffron threads

1 tablespoon milk

1 teaspoon caraway seeds

1 inch ginger, cut into thin strips

2 medium onions, sliced and deep-fried

½ cup chopped fresh mint leaves

2 tablespoons chopped fresh coriander

1 teaspoon screw pine water

1 teaspoon rose water

- Marinate the chicken in a mixture of ginger paste, garlic paste, green chilli paste, coriander powder, cumin powder, *garam masala* powder, cardamom powder, salt and yogurt for about half an hour.
- Heat one tablespoon of oil in a non-stick pan. Add the bay leaf, cloves, cardamoms and sauté for half a minute.
- Add the rice and sauté for a minute. Add the chicken stock and bring to a boil. Lower the heat and cook for eight to ten minutes or till the rice is three-fourth done. Drain and set aside.
- Soak the saffron in the milk.
- Heat the remaining oil in a thick-bottomed non-stick pan. Add the caraway seeds and sauté till fragrant.
- Add the marinated chicken and sauté for three to four minutes or till it is half cooked.
- Remove the pan from the heat. Spread the rice over the chicken.
- Sprinkle saffron-flavoured milk, ginger strips, fried onions, chopped mint and coriander, screw pine water and rose water over the rice.
- Cover and cook on *dum* for fifteen to twenty minutes over low heat.
- Serve hot with a *raita* of your choice.

Kongunadu Erachi Biryani

Mutton Biryani

500 grams mutton on the bone, cut into ½-inch pieces

1½ cups long-grained rice, soaked

½ teaspoon turmeric powder

Salt to taste

4 tablespoons oil + for deep-frying

2 onions, sliced thinly

½ cup grated coconut

8-10 black peppercorns

8 dried red chillies

1 tablespoon cumin seeds

1 tablespoon fennel seeds

2 tablespoons coriander seeds

1 tablespoon poppy seeds

1 inch ginger

12 garlic cloves

½ cup yogurt

2 bay leaves

4 green cardamoms

1 inch cinnamon

1 star anise

2 cloves

1 blade of mace

6 green chillies, slit

10-12 shallots, peeled

2 medium tomatoes, chopped

2 tablespoons chopped fresh mint

3 tablespoons chopped fresh coriander

1 tablespoon lemon juice

- Rub the turmeric powder and salt into the mutton pieces and set aside for fifteen minutes.
- Heat sufficient oil in a non-stick *kadai* and deep-fry the onions till golden brown. Drain on absorbent paper. Set aside.
- Dry-roast the coconut, peppercorns, red chillies, cumin seeds, fennel seeds, coriander seeds, poppy seeds, ginger and garlic, one by one, till fragrant.
- Cool and grind to a smooth paste with the yogurt.
- Wash the mutton thoroughly and parboil in four cups of water. Drain and reserve both the meat and the water.
- Heat four tablespoons of oil in a heavy-bottomed non-stick *handi*; add the bay leaves, cardamoms, cinnamon, star anise, cloves, mace and green chillies and sauté till fragrant.
- Add the shallots and sauté till light brown. Add the mutton and stir-fry over high heat till the edges start browning. Add the tomatoes and stir.
- Add the ground paste, lower the heat and sauté till the oil separates.
- Add two cups of the reserved mutton stock and cook over low heat for ten minutes.

- Add the soaked rice, the remaining mutton stock and salt to taste. Stir well and cook till the rice is three-fourth done.
- Sprinkle the browned onions, chopped mint and coriander over the rice and drizzle with the lemon juice.
- Cover the *handi* with a tight-fitting lid and place on hot charcoals, with a few burning charcoals on the lid as well. Cook for ten to fifteen minutes.
- Remove the lid when ready to serve.

Chef's Tip

You can make this *biryani* with chicken, boiled eggs or minced mutton balls.

PAELLA

1½ cups paella rice (or any short-grained rice), soaked

20-25 medium prawns

2 medium tomatoes, chopped

1 small red capsicum, cut into thin strips

1 medium green capsicum, cut into thin strips

200 grams chicken on the bone, cut into 1-inch pieces

6-8 squid, cut into rings

10-12 clams or mussels

¼ cup shelled green peas, blanched

½ cup olive oil

1 bay leaf

1 medium onion, sliced

3 garlic cloves, sliced

2 teaspoons paella spice mix

A few threads of saffron

3½ cups Chicken Stock (page 93)

Salt to taste

2 chicken stock cubes

Garnish

5-6 whole prawns, boiled

5-6 clams, boiled

2 lemons, cut into wedges

- Drain the soaked rice and set aside. Peel half the prawns and leave the heads on the rest.
- Heat the olive oil in a paella pan or a large non-stick frying pan.
- Add the bay leaf, onion and garlic and sauté till translucent. Add tomatoes and capsicums and stir well to mix.
- Add the chicken, squid, whole prawns, clams or mussels and mix well.
- Stir in the paella spice mix and saffron. Add the stock, salt and rice and mix again.
- Add the stock cubes, peeled prawns and green peas and cook till the rice is done.
- Garnish with boiled prawns and clams and serve hot with lemon wedges.

Chef's Tip

Paella spice mix is made with paprika, which is a mildly hot chilli powder and yellow food colour.

Nasi Lamek

1 cup rice, soaked
Oil for deep-frying
4 tablespoons peanuts
2 inches lemon grass stalk, chopped
1 inch ginger, sliced
2 shallots, sliced
2 cups coconut milk
Salt to taste
1 medium cucumber, sliced
2 eggs, boiled and sliced

- Heat plenty of oil in a non-stick wok and deep-fry the peanuts till golden brown.
- Drain on absorbent paper. Set aside.
- Place the rice in a clay (earthenware) pot; add the lemon grass, ginger, shallots and coconut milk. (If the coconut milk is too thick add a little water.)
- Add the salt and cook over high heat till the mixture comes to a boil.
- Lower the heat, cover and cook till the rice is tender.
- Serve hot with fried peanuts, slices of cucumber and boiled eggs.

Risotto Con Gamberi

Risotto with Prawns

1½ cups arborio rice
20 (300 grams) medium prawns
1 carrot, sliced
1 celery stalk, chopped
1 medium onion, sliced
5-6 black peppercorns
4 tablespoons butter
2 shallots, finely chopped
2-3 garlic cloves
1 tablespoon chopped fresh mixed herbs
3 tablespoons tomato purée
Salt to taste
10-12 black peppercorns, crushed
½ cup cream
2 tablespoons grated Parmesan cheese

- Pour five cups of water into a deep non-stick pan; add the carrot, celery, onion and peppercorns and bring to a boil.
- Add the prawns and boil for five minutes; drain. Reserve the stock, remove the prawns and discard the vegetables.
- Peel the prawns and slice in half lengthways, removing the dark vein along the back. Reserve four prawns for garnishing.
- Heat the butter in a non-stick pan; add the shallots, garlic and herbs and cook till golden brown.
- Add the rice and sauté for two to three minutes till well coated with butter.

- Stir in the tomato purée and cook for two minutes; add the prepared stock. Season with salt and crushed peppercorns and simmer till the rice is cooked.
- Gently mix in the prawns and the cream.
- Serve hot, garnished with whole prawns and grated Parmesan cheese.

Chef's Tip

The traditional method of cooking risotto is to add half a cup of hot stock at a time. When each portion of stock has been absorbed, more is added.

Macher Pulao

500 grams boneless fish (*rohu*), cut into 1-inch pieces

1½ cups rice, soaked

½ teaspoon turmeric powder

Salt to taste

2 tablespoons coriander seeds

6 dried red chillies, broken in half

1 teaspoon cumin seeds

6 cloves

4 tablespoons chopped fresh coriander

1 inch ginger

5 tablespoons ghee

Oil for deep-frying

2 large onions, sliced

- Pat the fish dry. Rub in the turmeric powder and salt and set aside.
- Dry-roast the coriander seeds on a non-stick *tawa*.
- Grind together the coriander seeds, red chillies, cumin seeds, cloves, chopped coriander and ginger to a fine paste.
- Heat three tablespoons of ghee in a non-stick pan; sauté the ground *masala* till the moisture evaporates and it turns a light red colour.
- Heat sufficient oil in a non-stick *kadai* and deep-fry the marinated fish. Drain on absorbent paper.

- Add the fish to the cooked *masala* with salt. Add two cups of water and cook, covered, for two minutes, or till the fish is tender.
- Remove the fish from the pan with a slotted spoon and keep warm. Set the gravy aside.
- Heat the remaining ghee in a deep non-stick pan and sauté the onions till light brown.
- Remove with a slotted spoon and drain on absorbent paper.
- Add the rice and salt to taste to the ghee remaining in the pan and mix well.
- Pour in the reserved fish gravy and one and a half cups of water; cook, covered over medium heat till the rice is cooked and the water has been absorbed.
- Arrange the fish pieces on top of the rice, cover and cook over low heat for five minutes.
- Serve hot.

Basic Recipes

Chicken Stock

Boil 200 grams chicken bones in water for 5 minutes. Drain and discard water. Boil blanched bones with a roughly chopped carrot, celery stalk, leek, 2-3 parsley stalks, 6-7 black peppercorns, 5-6 cloves, 1 bay leaf and 10 cups of water.

Remove any scum which rises to the surface and replace it with more cold water. Simmer for at least 1 hour. Remove from heat, strain, cool and store in a refrigerator till further use.

Chilli Oil

Cook 6 tablespoons of chopped dried red chillies in 1¼ cups of groundnut oil on low heat for at least ten minutes. When completely cold, stir in 2-3 tablespoons of red chilli powder and 1-2 tablespoons of sesame oil. Cover and leave to stand for at least twelve hours. Strain into a sterilised bottle and store in a cool, dark place.

Coconut Milk

Process 1 cup grated fresh coconut in a blender with ¼ cup warm water. Pass the ground coconut through a piece of muslin or strainer pressing firmly to extract all the juice, or first milk. Add a ¼ cup of warm water to the strained coconut to get the second, thinner milk from the same solids.

Green Chutney

Grind together 1 cup fresh coriander, ½ cup fresh mint, 2-3 green chillies, black salt to taste, ¼ teaspoon sugar and 1 tablespoon lemon juice to a smooth paste using a little water if required.

Red Curry Paste

Pound together 10 dried, seeded, soaked and drained long red chillies, a large pinch of salt, 1½ tablespoons chopped galangal, 3 tablespoons chopped lemon grass, 2 teaspoons grated kaffir lime rind, 1 tablespoon chopped fresh coriander roots, 1 tablespoon chopped red shallots and 2 tablespoons chopped garlic with a pestle and mortar, to a smooth paste. Alternatively grind all the ingredients together in a grinder till smooth.

Makes half a cup of curry paste.

Thai Green Curry Paste

Grind together 10 green chillies, 3 shallots, 9 garlic cloves, 1-inch galangal, 3-inch lemon grass stalk, ¼ teaspoon grated lemon rind, a small bunch of coriander roots, 2 teaspoons coriander seeds, 2 teaspoons cumin seeds and salt to taste to make a fine paste.

Vegetable Stock

Peel, wash and chop 1 onion, ½ medium carrot, 2-3 inch celery stalk and 2-3 garlic cloves. Place in a non-stick pan with 1 bay leaf, 5-6 peppercorns, 2-3 cloves and 5 cups of water and bring to a boil. Lower heat and simmer for 15 minutes and strain. Cool and store in a refrigerator till further use.

GLOSSARY

English	Hindi
Almonds	Badam
Asafoetida	Hing
Bay leaves	Tej patta
Bean sprouts	Ankurit moong
Bengal gram, split	Chana dal
Black gram, skinless split	Dhuli udad dal
Bottle gourd	Lauki
Brinjal	baingan
Cabbage	Patta gobhi
Capsicum	Shimla mirch
Caraway seeds	Shahi jeera
Cardamom, black	Badi elaichi
Cardamom, green	Chhoti elaichi
Carrots	Gajar
cashew nuts	Kaju

English	Hindi
Cauliflower	Phool gobhi
Celery	Ajmud
Chillies, red dried	Sookhi lal mirch
Chillies, red fresh	Taaze lal mirch
Cinnamon	Dalchini
Cloves	Laung
Coconut, fresh	Nariyal
Coriander seeds	Dhania
Corn kernels	Makai ke daane
Crabs	Kekda
Cream	Malai
Cucumber	Kakdi
Cumin seeds	Jeera
Curry leaves	Kadhi patta
Fennel seeds	Badi saunf
Fenugreek seeds	Methi dana

English	Hindi
Green peas	Hare matar
Honey	Shahad
Mace	Javitri
Mint	Pudina
Mushroom	Khumb
Mussels	Seepee
Mustard seeds	Rai
Nutmeg	Jaiphal
Orange	Santara
Peanuts	Moong phalli
Peppercorns, black	Kali mirch
Pineapple	Ananas
Poppy seeds	Khus khus
Prawns	Jheenga

English	Hindi
Raisins	Kishmish
Rose water	Gulab jal
Saffron	Kesar
Screw pine water	Kewra jal
Sesame seed	Til
Shallots	Chhote pyaaz
Spinach	Palak
Squid	Samudra pheni
Star anise	Chakri phool
Tamarind	Imli
Turmeric	Haldi
Turmeric, fresh	Taazi haldi
Vinegar	Sirka
Yogurt	Dahi